First Edition
Genuine Autographed Collectible

Do you want me to sign it in ink or in lipstick?

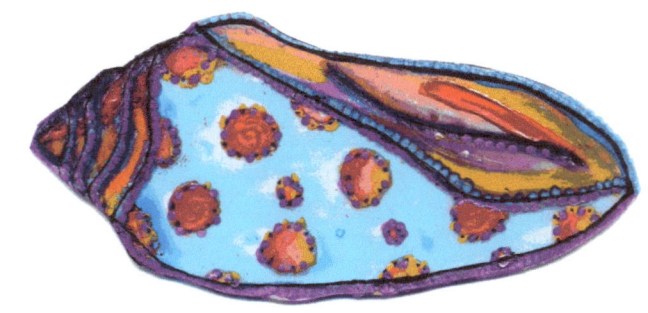

A Gift of Beach Bum Poetry

Gift Card

Date:

To:

From:

Message:

What Do Books Do?

BOOKS ARE POWERFUL!

Books Educate!

Book Enlighten!

Books Empower!

Books Emancipate!

Books Entertain!

Books Spring Eternal!

Books Drive Exploration!

Books Spark Evolution!

Books Ignite Revolution!

Sharon Esther Lampert

Gift Shop: BooksArePowerful.com

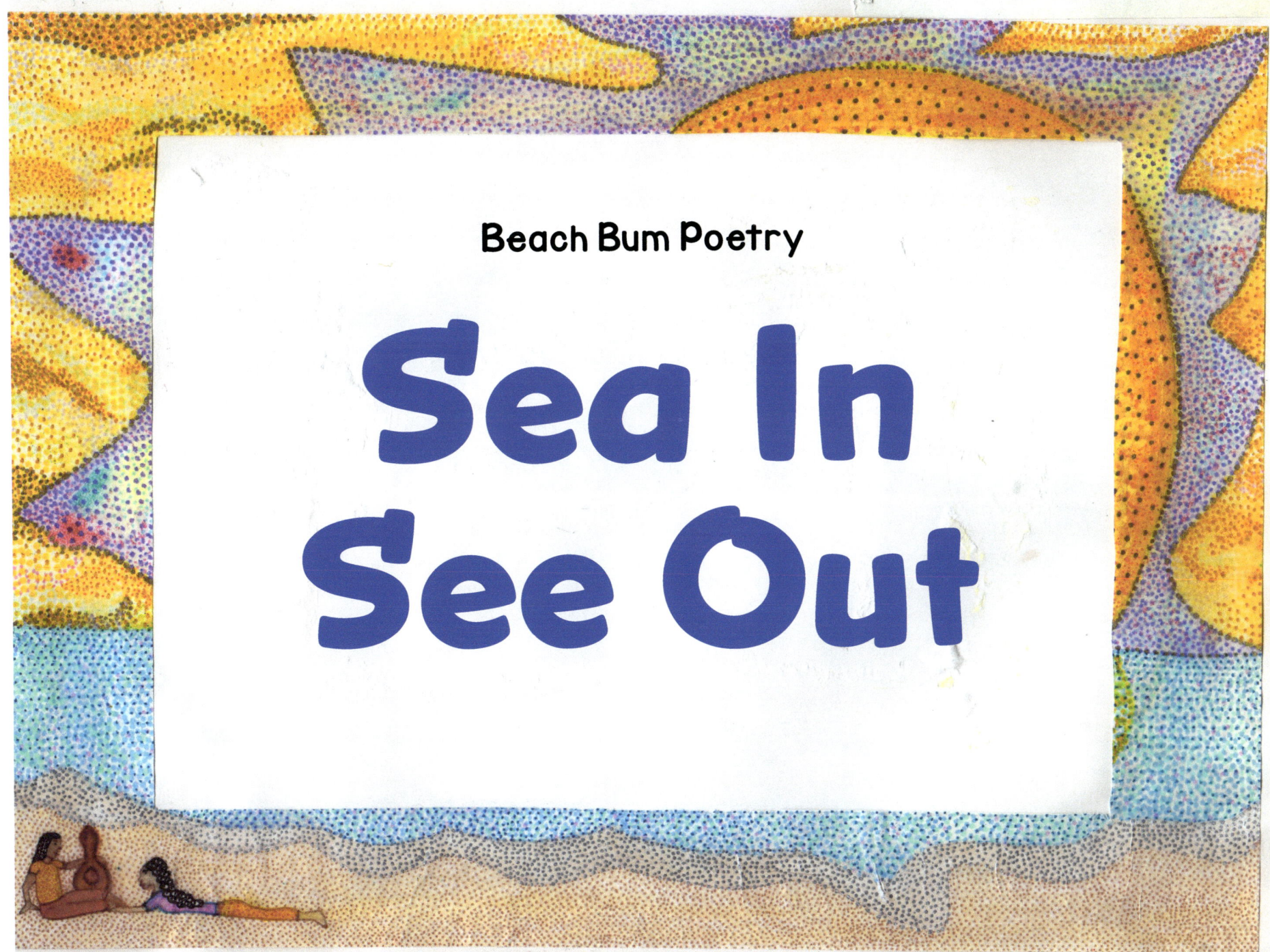

Literature, Poetry, Beach, Rockaway Beach, Genius, Sharon Esther Lampert

SEA IN SEE OUT Beach Bum Poetry

©2022 by Sharon Esther Lampert. All Rights Reserved. No part of this book may be used or reproduced in any manner whatsoever without written permission except in the case of brief quotations embodied in critical articles and reviews.

KADIMAH PRESS: GIFTS OF GENIUS

Books may be purchased for education, business, or sales promotional use.
ISBN: Hardcover 978-1-885872-60-9
Library of Congress Control Number: 2022911021

Palm Beach Book Publisher
www.PalmBeachBookPublisher.com
Phone: 917-767-5843
FAN MAIL: FANS@SharonEstherLampert.com
Website: www.SharonEstherLampert.com

Book Design and Interior Creative Genius Sharon Esther Lampert
Illustrations: Kim Colwell
Editor: Dave Segal

Global Online Websites for Orders and Distribution:
Ingram, 1 Ingram Blvd. La Vergne, TN 37086-3629
Phone: 615-793-5000
Fax orders: 615-287-6990

First Edition

Manufactured in the United States of America

Age 9:
"My daughter is a poet, philosopher, and teacher.
Sharon is the Princess & the Pea!
THE QUEEN HAS ARRIVED!
BEAUTY & BRAINS!"
XOXO
—MOMMY

Beach Bum Poetry

Sea In See Out

Sharon Esther Lampert
Author

Kim Colwell
Illustrator

Palm Beach Book Publisher
Florida

Beach Bum Poetry Inspiration

May the sun-baked sands warm the cool bare bottoms
of your two gallant feet and boldy-yet
oh so gently tempt, touch, and tickle your
ten adventurous toes to bravely
take you on beach bum poetry journey-
fearlessly into the infinite depths of your imagination
where magic and memory mix a poet's brew of literary prowess,
and way daring, way dauntless, and way deeper
courageously into the hearty creative crevices
containing pure feelings of your own special soul
to inspire a whole summer of beach bum poetry
to last a whole winter through... and perhaps a lifetime too!

-Sharon Esther Lampert, Beach Bum

Table of Contents

Rockaway Beach – My Backyard

The Restless Sunrise ... p. 1

Sun Love ... p. 2

Saucy Seagulls ... p. 3

Sea In, Sea Out ... p. 4

Swifty Sandcrabs ... p. 5

Sky-High Sandcastles ... pp. 6-7

The Perfect SeaShell ... p. 8

Sunset City ... p. 9

Moon-Mad Rhythms ... p. 10

A Star's Afterglow ... p. 11

Poetry Education for Beach Bums ... pp. 12-13

SEE THE WORLD THROUGH THE EYES OF A CREATIVE GENIUS .. pp. 14-15

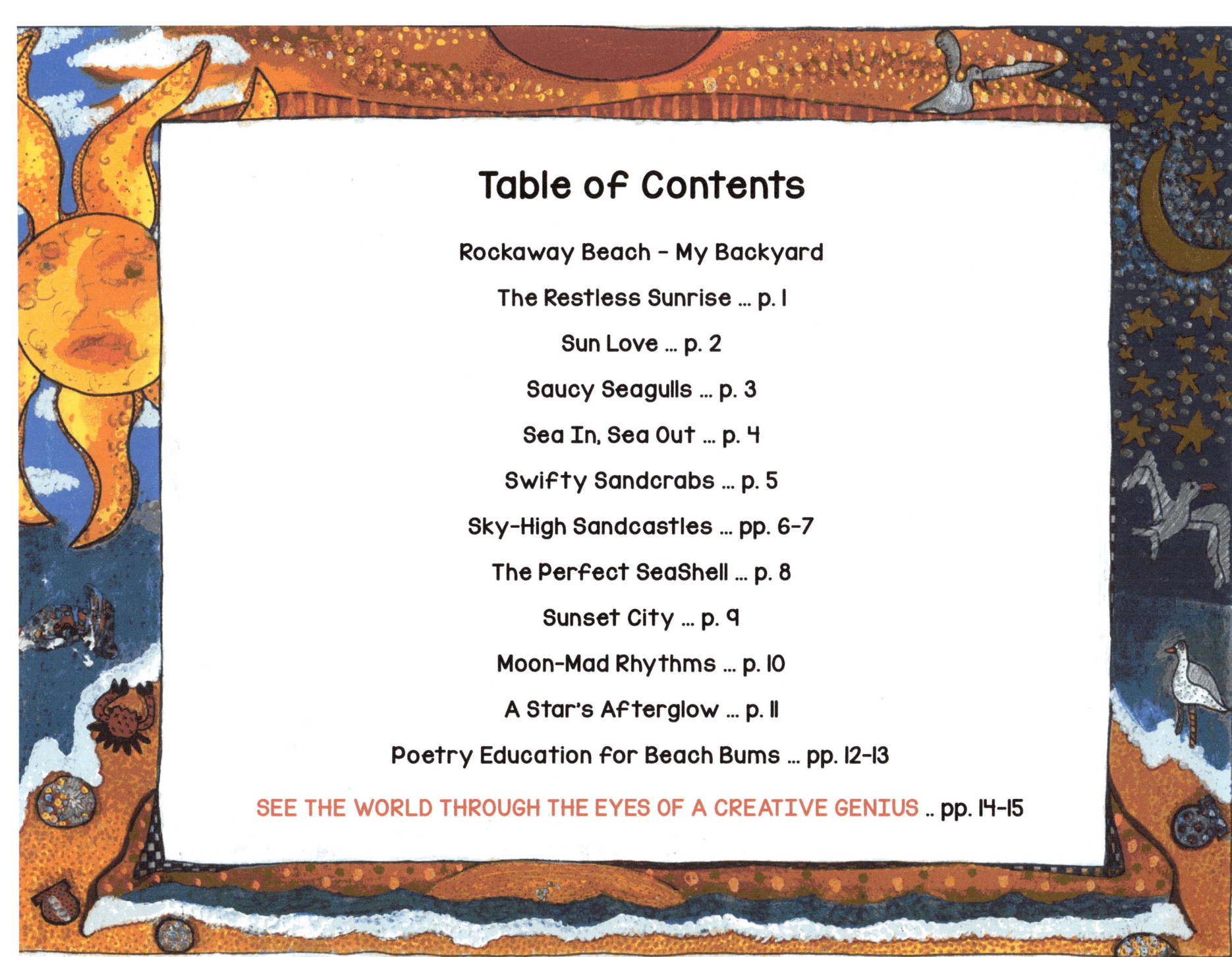

Age 9:
"My daughter is a Poet, Philosopher, and Teacher. My daughter is the Princess & Pea!"

Beauty & Brains!
LOVE & XOXO
—MOMMY

Rockaway Beach

By Sharon Esther Lampert

There is a serene aura that surrounds my hometown.
This is attributable to the beautiful blue-green waters of the Atlantic Ocean.
The brisk, flow of sea water sprays into the atmosphere.
It leaves behind traces of residue in the air..
The ocean waves rush back and forth
covering the footprints of the web footed seagulls embedded in the sand .
And of any trace of mankind.

The undercurrents of the waves have scattered
a mass of many multicolored sea organisms;
oyster, clam, and mussel shells along the shore.
There are also remnants of crab skeletons and jellyfish.
...They are found nearby a decayed wooden jetty.
Sandwiched inbetween the shells is an abundance of slimy green algae.
And attached to the outside of the shells are barnacles and thick green seaweed.

The setting sun resembles a yellow beach ball enclosed in a fiery red ring.
This casts a reflection over the water's surface
triggering it to sparkle like a bursting firecracker.
The setting sun slowly sinks into the water and behind the clouds,
Across the horizon remains a purplish, silver lining .

As the moon rises, it is high tide and the water shelters the seashells like a blanket.
The shadow of the moon on the surface of the water, spotlights a resting seagull.
His wings are curled beneath his body and his head tucked under his chin.
In the distance, one can hear the squawking of the seagulls.
They soar through the blue sky, encircling the sun.
A seagull descends onto the glossy surface of the water,
swiftly gliding across the rippling waves.
He perches himself on a rotted wooden jetty,
unruffles his wet feathers and gulps down his prey.
A cool breeze has just begun to set in,
giving the sand a chilling sensation, when touched.

Is there a remote place in this universe where harmony and tranquility exists?

Yes there is. In **Rockaway Beach.**

In 1985, my beloved MOMMY passed away. I found my poem among her belongings. There was no date on it.

I think... I wrote this poem when I was in high school.

MOMMY had taken the poem to her office where she had a copy machine.

MOMMY made 50 COPIES of my poem! Only a MOMMY would do that!

Today, my ardent fans make copies of my poems and pass them out to family and friends.

Sea In, See Out

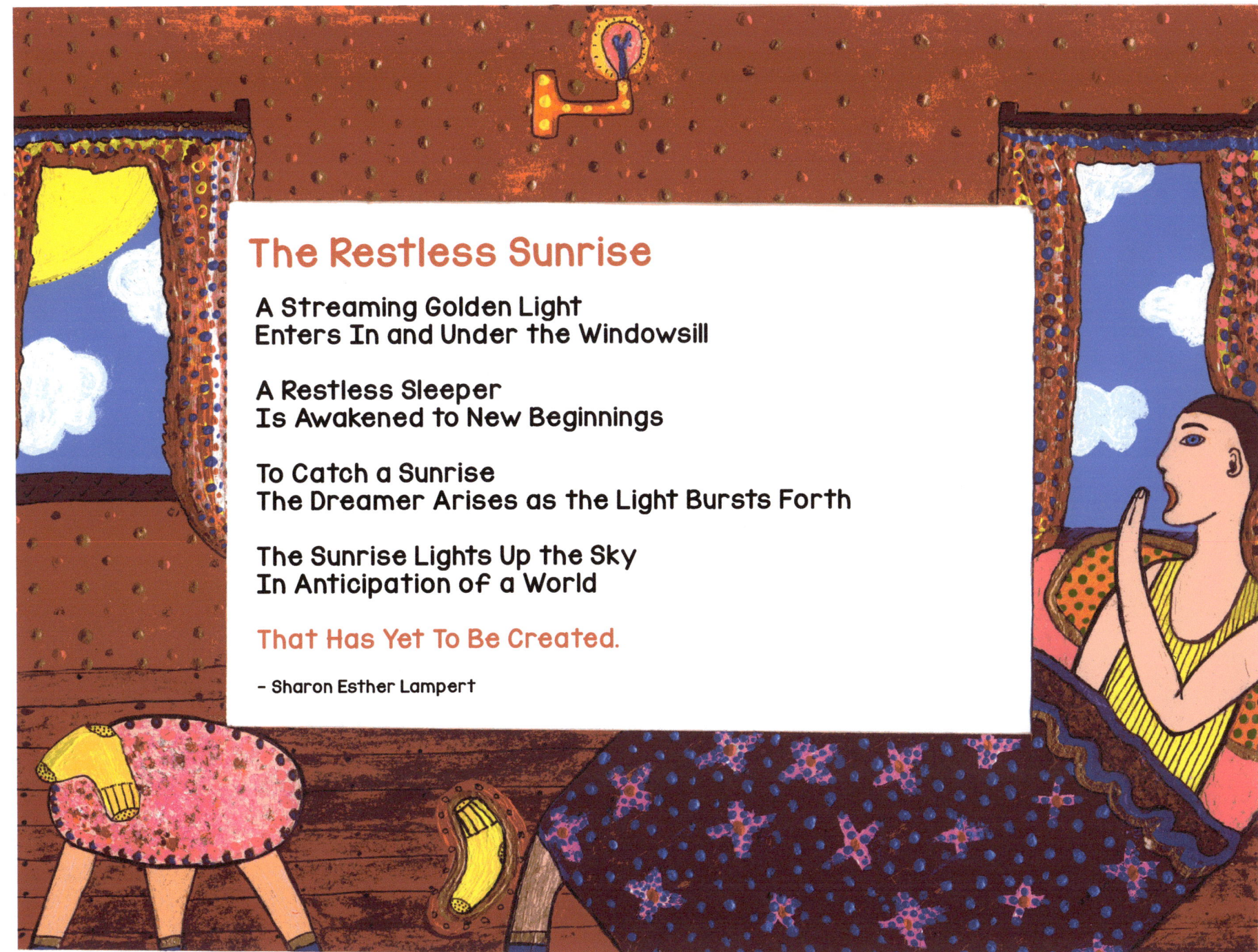

The Restless Sunrise

A Streaming Golden Light
Enters In and Under the Windowsill

A Restless Sleeper
Is Awakened to New Beginnings

To Catch a Sunrise
The Dreamer Arises as the Light Bursts Forth

The Sunrise Lights Up the Sky
In Anticipation of a World

That Has Yet To Be Created.

– Sharon Esther Lampert

Sun Love

The loving light of the shimmering sun brings
a jumping joy to the effervescent earth

Dozens of dazzling seagulls dance into and
out of the plush whispering-white clouds charmingly
laced together in the streaming-forever sky

The sparkling-kinetic sea touchingly twinkles
as the charismatic-sun caresses

Generously, the mellow-mesmerizing sun
warms the grainy grand-sandy seashore

Precocious children build sophisticated sandcastles of classic
and contemporary design. The modern skycrapers and ancient
medieval castles longingly lean toward the sun

The sun's lovely, lively, and lush radiating rays penetrate deeply
and deliciously, organically empowering as soul-energy, and
inorganically empowering as solar energy.

The splendid sun embraces all living inhabitants and all non-living things.

–Sharon Esther Lampert, Beach Bum

Sea In, See Out

Saucy Seagulls

Free floating in the forever heavens, wings are stretched worldwide.
Serenading seagulls squeal and squawk, eyeing the tide

Up above, across the boundless streams of satin-n-silk sapphire-blue sky
Daringly encircling the furiously-hot soft-spoken sun,
saucy seagulls sizzle by.

Down below, in the slick seams where the wet sea meets the dry sky
Seagulls gracefully glide, sailing across the cool-rippling crescents,
cravings they cry! Navigating glassy, glossy, and glitzy
surfaces of wavering waves, empty bellies, they try!

Landing, a lone seagull languidly decends...

Perfectly perching, on a rare space of a rotted-wooden jetty,
a testy-encrusted tightrope, meaty-muscles are stuck together
clasped ever-so closed, despite, there is hope!

Famished, in split seconds, and thirds, down the hatch, "Gulp!" go
frightful-precious prey, fearless-feathers unruffle, consuming all...
conquest after conquest after conquest have no say!

The seagull graciously partakes of nature's unfathomable bounty

-Sharon Esther Lampert, Beach Bum

Sea in Sea Out

Sharon Esther Lampert

(1)
Lights On, Day In, Day Out,
Happy Harmony and Sweet Serenity
Captivates the Buoyant Beach of Bubbly Blue Sea.
Endlessly, Vacillating, Velvet and Vocal Waters
of Scintillating Sea Sprays into Infinite Air Spaces.
Trailing, Salty Traces of a Sweetly Soothing
Aroma – An Ambiance. Lights On, Night Out, Day In

(2)
Lights Out, Night In, Night Out,
Cohabiting, at Deepest Depths of Seemingly
Bottomless Overwhelming Ocean, in an
Organized Wilderness of Divine Decree are
Collector's Sassy Seashells and Culinary Edibles –
Delightful, Delicious and Delectable Delicacies.
Lights Out, Night In, Day Out

(3)
War On.
Awash is the Sea in a Bloodbath.
Lights On, Day In, Night Out, Day Out, Night In, Lights Out.
Blue Sea Water Bloodied Red By Sea Beasts Armed Bi Jaws.
Courageously Hungry,
       The Pains of Hunger
          Exact Pain from the
             Courageously Hunted
Salty, Salty, Sea Water – Tears of the Fallen.
Salty, Salty, Sea Water – Wounds of the Survivors Heal.
Devoured–
The Hunted Feel No More of Pain
and No More of Pleasure. Never.
Satiated–
the Hungry Feel Pleasure. Always.
War Out

(4)
Day In, Day Out, Lights On,
Lights Out, Night In, Night Out
Waves Rush Back with Quiet Tranquility
and Rage Forth with Brazen Abandon Covering
Furiously Fast and Fancy Footprint Trails of
Two By Two Webbed Footed Seagulls,
Four By Four Creepy Crawling Prey,
and of Any Trace of Humankind's
Flatfooted Trials and Tribulations

– Sharon Esther Lampert, Beach Bum

Sea In, See Out

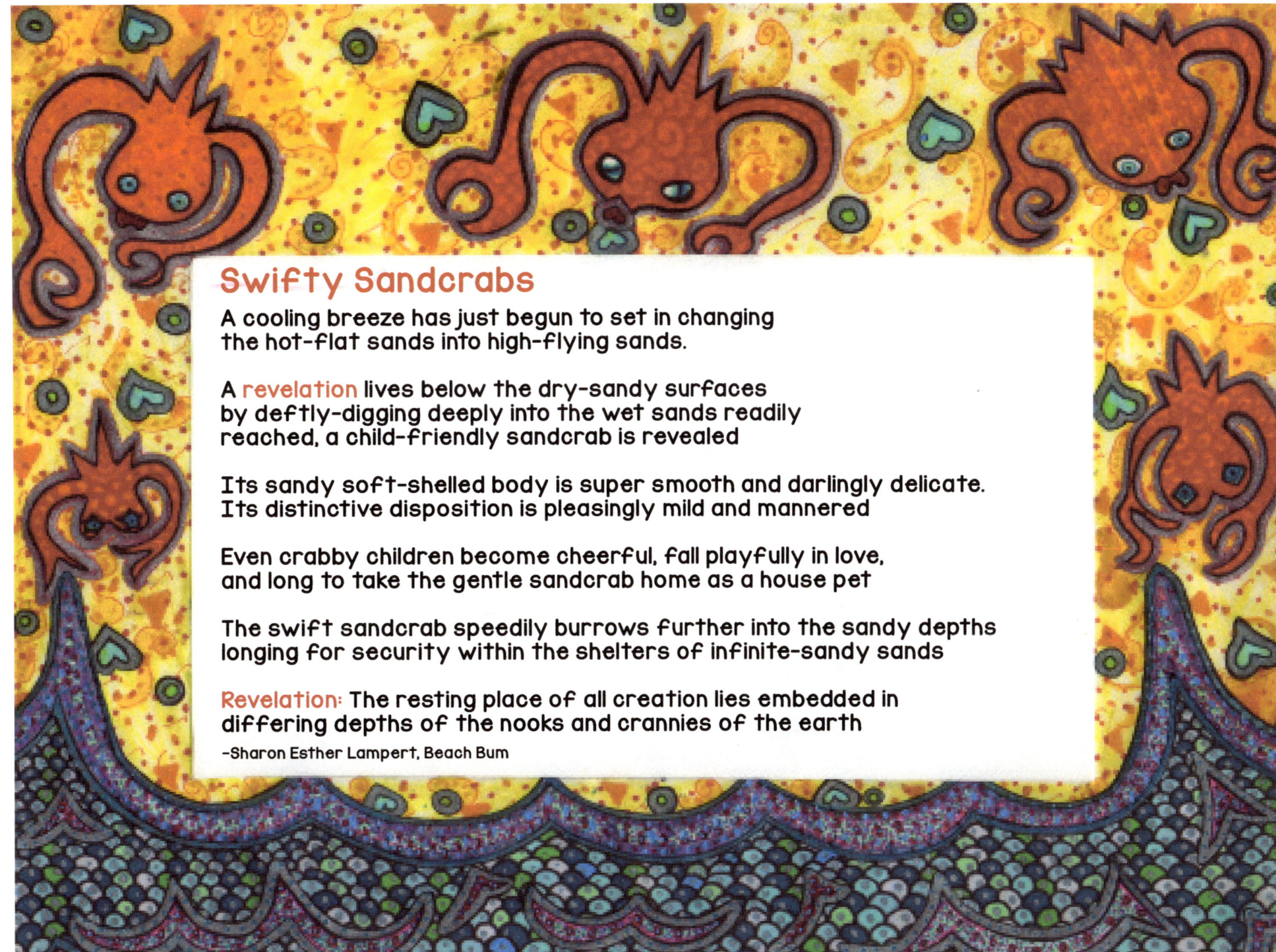

Swifty Sandcrabs

A cooling breeze has just begun to set in changing
the hot-flat sands into high-flying sands.

A revelation lives below the dry-sandy surfaces
by deftly-digging deeply into the wet sands readily
reached, a child-friendly sandcrab is revealed

Its sandy soft-shelled body is super smooth and darlingly delicate.
Its distinctive disposition is pleasingly mild and mannered

Even crabby children become cheerful, fall playfully in love,
and long to take the gentle sandcrab home as a house pet

The swift sandcrab speedily burrows further into the sandy depths
longing for security within the shelters of infinite-sandy sands

Revelation: The resting place of all creation lies embedded in
differing depths of the nooks and crannies of the earth

-Sharon Esther Lampert, Beach Bum

Sky High Sand Castles

In a fragile moment of time:
A sandcastle reaches ever upward, toward the great, glorious and gargantuan sun, sandy, and sky high, seemingly strong when packed solid, and sturdy when packed wet

In a carefree moment of time:
Enticed by my sandwich, a steady, swift, and soaring wild seagull, lands on the sandy lighthouse's muddy-packed pinnacle.
To the apex, she crept and she crept, and she crept

In a sudden moment of time:
Delicately wet, harmless, a sun shower appears

In a magical moment of time:
Seemingly rare, dripless, a rainbow appears

Sea In, See Out

In an adventurous moment of time:
Rushing solely to roam, boundless, she reaches for the beckoning sky. She takes flight leaving behind faint, pristine-prissy prints in wet sand, she wrote

In a imagined moment of time:
She takes a direction, in the sky so dry, to follow the rainbow's trail, so very real and sky amplified. Seeing in as far as the mind's eye can imagine, seemingly myth & mystified, so very inviting of an alibi...

In a moment of time immortal:
May her radiating wings unknowingly posed, in my mind's eye beaming bright & brilliant, inspire enduring beach poetry of timeless beauty, rebirthed & reborn in time – eternally anew.

Sharon Esther Lampert, Beach Bum

The Perfect Seashell

Powerful undercurrents unseen by a forthcoming wave's determined surface, scatter masses upon masses upon masses of multi-ethnic sea organisms around and about

Weaving over and under the crusading-crashing surf nose-diving headless and heartless into the seashore, tailless horseshoe crabs, pearlless oysters, meatless clams, and mussels in a tussle, grope huggingly for underlying wet sands.

Sticky-stuck, green algae and slimy-gooey seaweed betwixt & between seashells: a muddle of sea puddle

The waves recede ...

Undamaged by the sea's rough & rugged undertoe,
A whole seashell rests on the shore
I pick up and pocket the perfect seashell
A lucky find and a miraculous wonder!

–Sharon Esther Lampert, Beach Bum

Sea In, See Out

Sunset City

The slowly sinking-setting sun falls into the cold sea

The sun descends into and out of and into and out of
the pillory and powdery clouds of chiffon drapery

Children in the midst of play return home, no longer free ...

Bewitchingly, a sunset becomes a bursting firecracker beaming,
and sparkling over the wet water's secure-surface streaming.

Lovers begin their embrace ...

Flagrantly painted across a sensational sacred skyline,
a yellowish-orange, redish-purple, and pinkish-silver
lace-lining lingers lightly, as a byline, designed & signed
by a mastermind, not of humankind

Forever spectacular is the memory of a sunset, each is one of a kind

-Sharon Esther Lampert, Beach Bum

Moon-Mad Rhythms

The rising moon lights up the nighty-night sky
At midnight, a magnificent moon-swept protective blanket of
blacketly-black shiny sea shelters the slumbering sleepers
and deep dreamers of the cosmopolitan sea world

Majestic waves of euphonic waters vibrate vacantly
serenely back and smashingly forth to resounding
beckoning and beseeching moon-mad rhythms

Moonlighting, awaiting the morning music of
melodious serenades, from moon-crooning ministering
seagulls of marvelous pitches come a swooning

Moonbeams spotlight a starlet of a seagull
Silently, she sleeps securely, cocooning.
The moonlight becomes her

—Sharon Esther Lampert, Beach Bum

Sea In, See Out

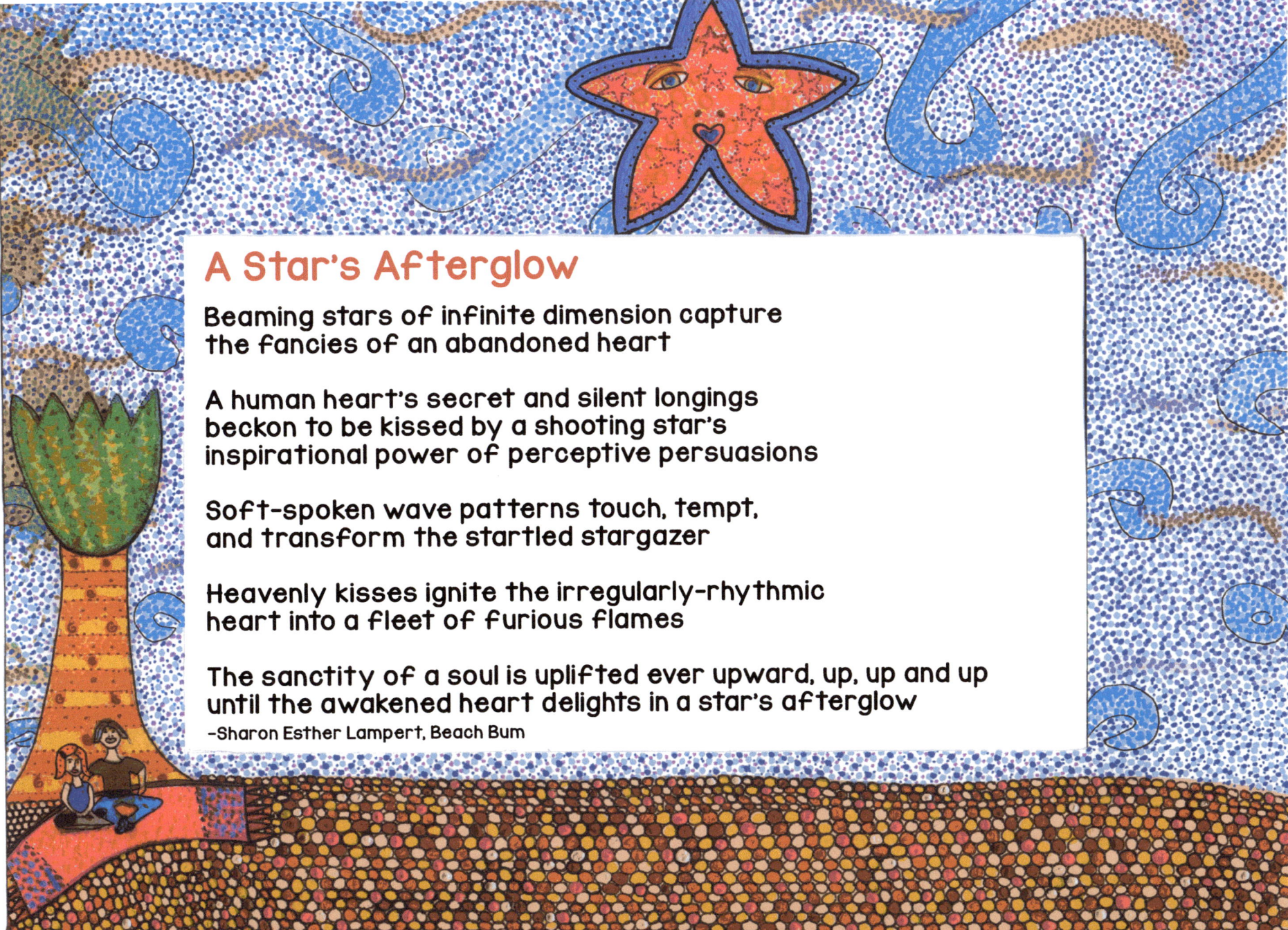

A Star's Afterglow

Beaming stars of infinite dimension capture
the fancies of an abandoned heart

A human heart's secret and silent longings
beckon to be kissed by a shooting star's
inspirational power of perceptive persuasions

Soft-spoken wave patterns touch, tempt,
and transform the startled stargazer

Heavenly kisses ignite the irregularly-rhythmic
heart into a fleet of furious flames

The sanctity of a soul is uplifted ever upward, up, up and up
until the awakened heart delights in a star's afterglow

–Sharon Esther Lampert, Beach Bum

Rhythm Patterns in Poetry

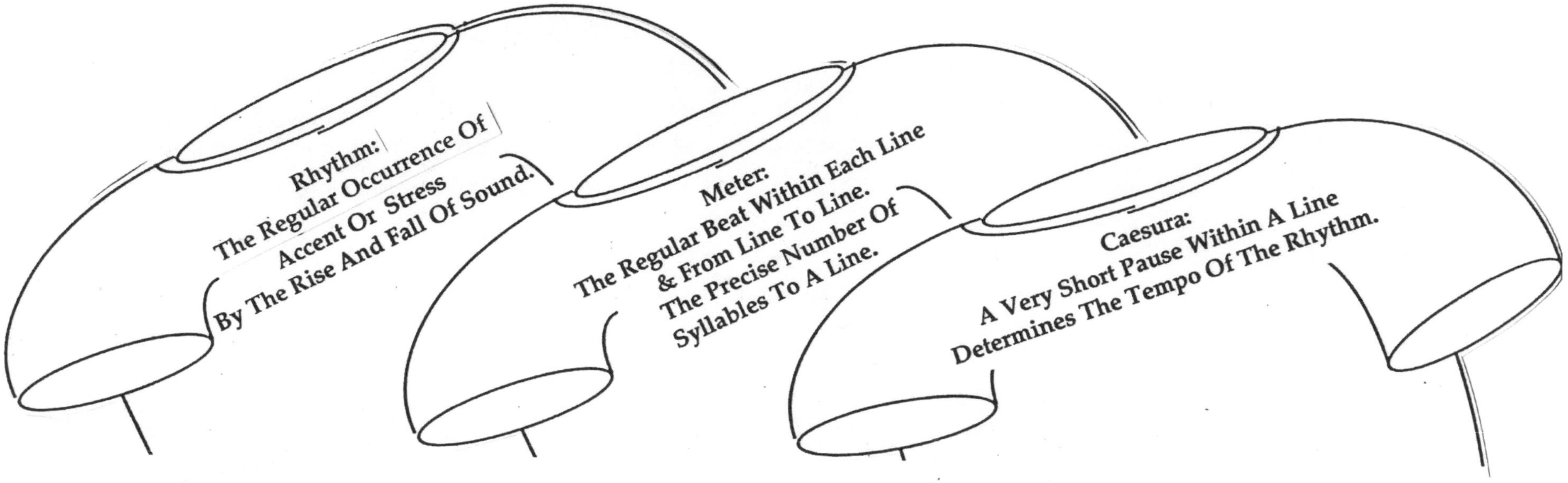

Rhythm: The Regular Occurrence Of Accent Or Stress By The Rise And Fall Of Sound.

Meter: The Regular Beat Within Each Line & From Line To Line. The Precise Number Of Syllables To A Line.

Caesura: A Very Short Pause Within A Line Determines The Tempo Of The Rhythm.

Developed Word Patterns Bring to the Listener the Music of a Poem

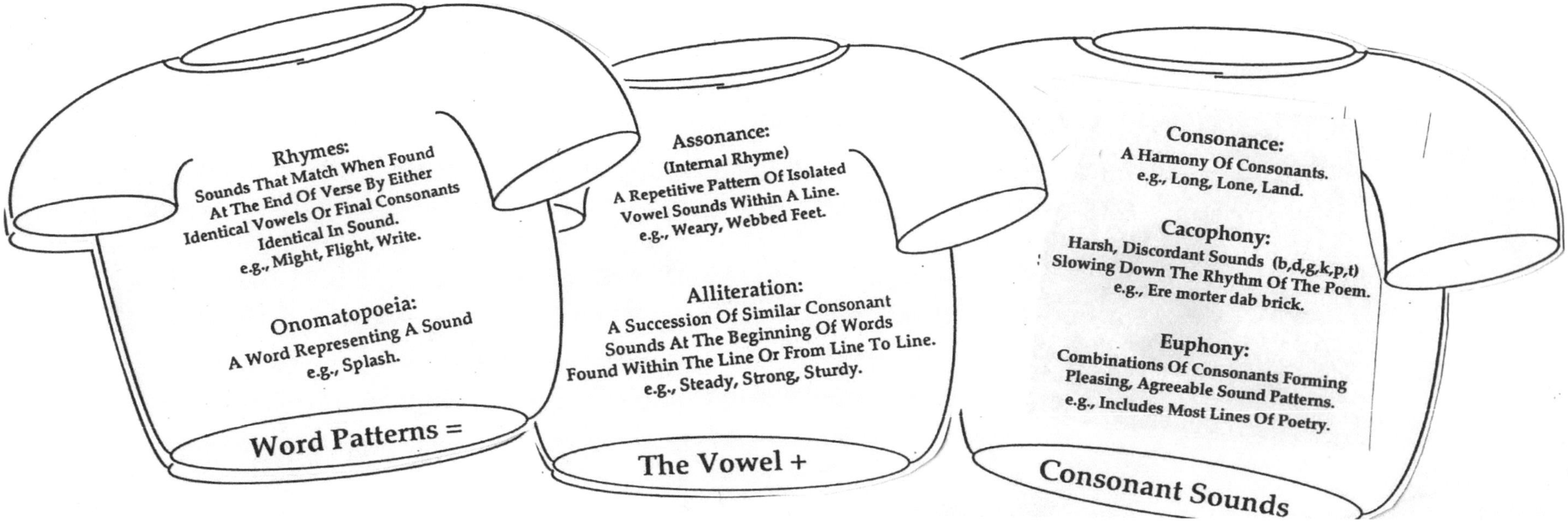

Rhymes: Sounds That Match When Found At The End Of Verse By Either Identical Vowels Or Final Consonants Identical In Sound. e.g., Might, Flight, Write.

Onomatopoeia: A Word Representing A Sound e.g., Splash.

Assonance: (Internal Rhyme) A Repetitive Pattern Of Isolated Vowel Sounds Within A Line. e.g., Weary, Webbed Feet.

Alliteration: A Succession Of Similar Consonant Sounds At The Beginning Of Words Found Within The Line Or From Line To Line. e.g., Steady, Strong, Sturdy.

Consonance: A Harmony Of Consonants. e.g., Long, Lone, Land.

Cacophony: Harsh, Discordant Sounds (b,d,g,k,p,t) Slowing Down The Rhythm Of The Poem. e.g., Ere morter dab brick.

Euphony: Combinations Of Consonants Forming Pleasing, Agreeable Sound Patterns. e.g., Includes Most Lines Of Poetry.

Word Patterns = The Vowel + Consonant Sounds

Sea In, See Out

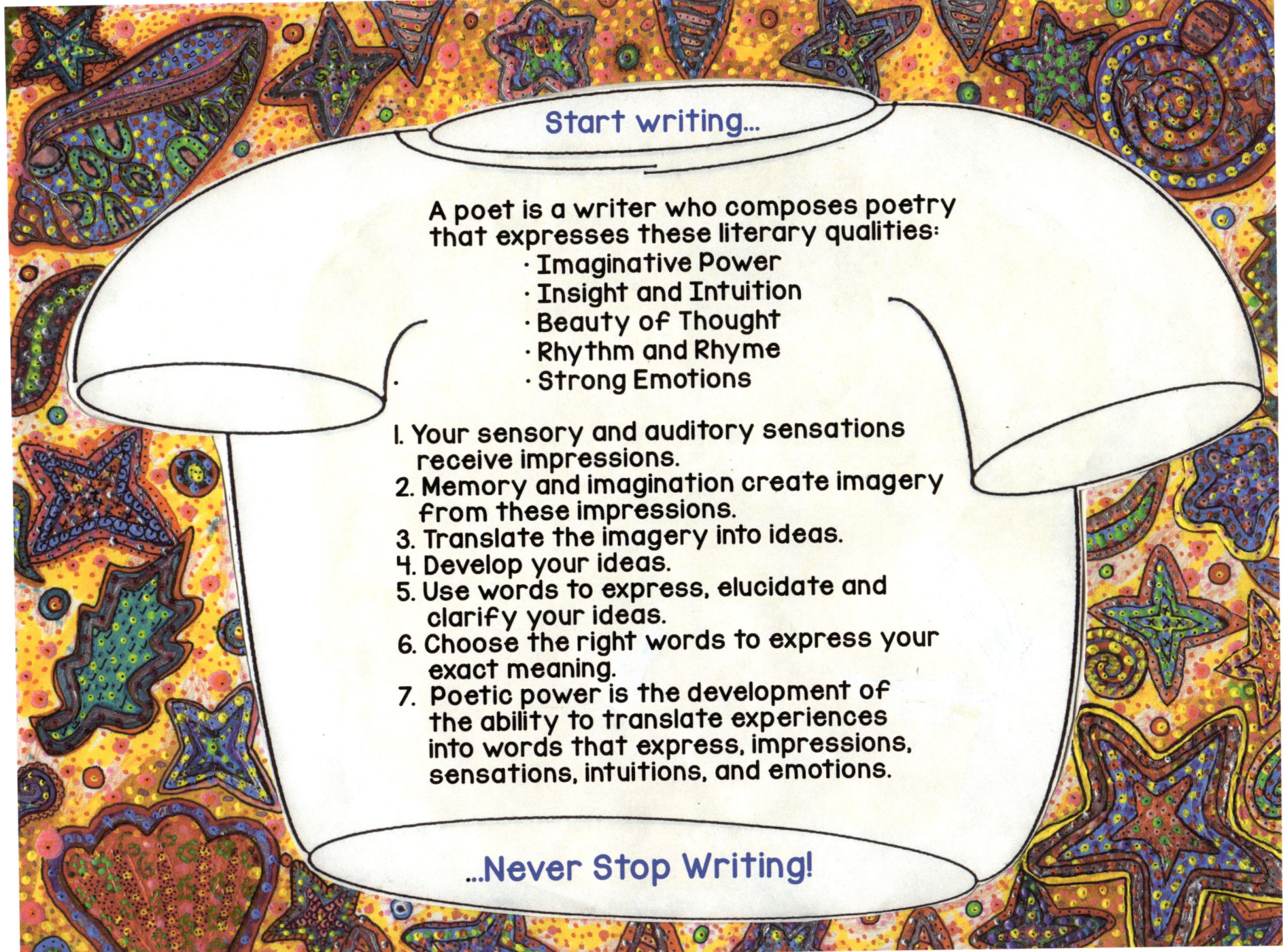

Start writing...

A poet is a writer who composes poetry that expresses these literary qualities:
- Imaginative Power
- Insight and Intuition
- Beauty of Thought
- Rhythm and Rhyme
- Strong Emotions

1. Your sensory and auditory sensations receive impressions.
2. Memory and imagination create imagery from these impressions.
3. Translate the imagery into ideas.
4. Develop your ideas.
5. Use words to express, elucidate and clarify your ideas.
6. Choose the right words to express your exact meaning.
7. Poetic power is the development of the ability to translate experiences into words that express, impressions, sensations, intuitions, and emotions.

...Never Stop Writing!

Sharon Esther Lampert

SEE THE WORLD THROUGH THE EYES OF A CREATIVE GENIUS

* Poet
* Prophet
* Philosopher
* Peacemaker
* Princess & Pea
* PINUP
* Performer: Vocalist
* Player: Jock
* Paladin of Education
* PHOTON SUPERHERO
* Princess Kadimah
* President
* Publisher
* Producer
* Psychobiologist
* Piano-Playing Cat
* Phoenix
* Prodigy

24 Websites:

SharonEstherLampert.com
PhilosopherQueen.com
WorldFamousPoems.com
VeryExtraSpecial.com
PoetryJewels.com
PoetryEssentialService.com
10Miracles.com
GodofWhat.com
Schmaltzy.com
TrueLoveBurnsEternal.com
SillyLittleBoys.com
Smartgrades.com
EverydayanEasyA.com
PhotonSuperHero.com
BooksNotBombs.com
PlannerParExcellence.com
FloridaRetirementPlanner.com
WritersRunTheWorld.com
PalmBeachBookPublisher.com

Gift Shop: GodIsGoDo.com
Gift Shop: HappyGrandparenting.com
Gift Shop: ArtHeart.store
Gift Shop: WorldPeaceEquation.com
Gift Shop: BooksArePowerful.com

NYU

Honored
Sharon Lampert
with an Award for

Multi-Interdisciplinary Studies
(YOUTUBE video)

Sharon was also honored to represent her M.A. class at her NYU graduation
(YOUTUBE video)

Sea In, See Out

About the Pr**od**i**g**y
SHARON ESTHER LAMPERT
V.E.S.S.E.L. **V**ery. **E**xtra. **S**pecial. **S**haron. **E**sther. **L**ampert.

POET—"A LIST" One of the World's Greatest Poets
The Greatest Poems Ever Written on Extraordinary World Events
http://famouspoetsandpoems.com/poets.html

PROPHET
The 22 Commandments: All You Will Ever Need to Know About God

PHILOSOPHER QUEEN
- God Talks to Me: A Working Definition of God **GOD IS GO! DO!**
- God of What? Is Life a Gift or a Punishment? 18 Absolute Truths

PEACEMAKER
World Peace Equation.com

PHOTON
SUPERHERO OF EDUCATION

PALADIN OF EDUCATION
SMARTGRADES BRAIN POWER REVOLUTION
- "The Silent Crisis Destroying America's Brightest Minds" BOOK OF THE MONTH
- EVERYDAY AN EASY A.com
- 40 Universal Gold Standards of Education
- 15 Stepping Stones of Academic Successs
- 15 Stumbling Blocks of Academic Failure

PRODIGY
- Unleash the Creator, The GOD Within:
  10 Esoteric Laws of Genius and Creativity
- SILLY LITTLE BOYS: 40 Rules of Manhood, www.SillyLittleBoys.com
- Sperm Manifesto: 10 Rules for the Road
- CUPID: The Language of Love—Written in Letter **C**
- Temporary Insanity—Written in Letter **S**
  We Are All Building Our Lives on a Sand Trap
- The Secret Sauce of Book Sales—Written in Letter **P**
- Win at Thin: Fat Me, Skinny Me—Written in Letter **A**

PINUP
SEXIEST CREATIVE GENIUS IN HUMAN HISTORY

Princess & Pea
Sharon Esther wakes up in the middle of the night, and writes a whole book.

Sharon Esther Lampert

I Am Mortal.
My Books Are Immortal.
Please Handle My Books Gently.
My Books Are My Remains.

This book was compiled in three parts.
Part 1. **Birth**—Childhood Poem: **"Rockaway Beach"**
1985: After my Mother's death, I found my poem
while sifting through her personal belongings.
I found 50 copies of my poem!
Part 2. Format Book—June 7-9, 2022
Part 3. Publish—August 15, 2022

Sharon Esther Lampert
SEE THE WORLD THROUGH THE EYES OF A CREATIVE GENIUS
Poet, **P**rophet, **P**hilosopher, **P**eacemaker, **P**rincess & **P**ea, **P**rodigy

www.ingramcontent.com/pod-product-compliance
Lightning Source LLC
Chambersburg PA
CBHW041644220426
43661CB00018B/1295